MW00635693

This book
belongs to:

A READER'S JOURNAL

Read, Remember, and Reflect On Your Favorite Books

Bookishly

A TarcherPerigee Book

tarcherperigee

an imprint of Penguin Random House LLC
penguinrandomhouse.com

Copyright © 2024 by Bookishly Limited
Penguin Random House supports copyright. Copyright fuels creativity, encourages
diverse voices, promotes free speech, and creates a vibrant culture. Thank you for
buying an authorized edition of this book and for complying with copyright laws
by not reproducing, scanning, or distributing any part of it in any form without
permission. You are supporting writers and allowing Penguin Random House to
continue to publish books for every reader.

Illustrations by Gemma Harbour and Jess Thomas

TarcherPerigee with tp colophon is a registered trademark of Penguin Random
House LLC

Most TarcherPerigee books are available at special quantity discounts for bulk
purchase for sales promotions, premiums, fundraising, and educational needs.
Special books or book excerpts also can be created to fit specific needs. For
details, write SpecialMarkets@penguinrandomhouse.com.

Trade paperback ISBN: 9780593713310

Printed in the United States of America
1st Printing

Hello!

Welcome to the book lover's
reading journal of your dreams!

At Bookishly, all we want is for everyone to live their best bookish life, whether that means whizzing through as many books as you can each year, or occasionally reflecting on what you read over no set time frame. This journal will help provide the structure for you to read as much or as little as you like over the months ahead.

There're 52 spaces for reflections, plus some fun and diverting activities to get you dreaming about your favorite books, genres, authors, and characters.

So dive in! Level up your bookish adventures into all the worlds reading takes us.

My Reading Profile

Fill this out at the start of the journal and again at the end when you've finished to see if anything has changed.

DATE:

MY FAVORITE BOOK:

_____

MY FAVORITE AUTHOR:

_____

MY FAVORITE GENRE:

_____

WHERE I READ:

_____

WHEN I READ:

_____

WHY I READ:

_____

Reading Goals

Is there anything you want to achieve
while you are filling out this journal?
Are you planning to try new genres, or to read
a certain number of books in a year?
There's no wrong answer!

_____
_____
_____
_____
_____
_____
_____
_____
_____
_____
_____
_____
_____

Book Log Prompts

Here're some ideas of things you might like to consider when filling out your journal.

What were your first impressions of the book?

Did they turn out to be right?

What character did you relate to the most? Why?

What did you enjoy the most about the book?

What was your favorite quote from the book?

What did you dislike?

Did you like the ending?

Did the author include characters from a **diverse** range of backgrounds?

What **privileges** did the characters have?

Did characters from (marginalized) communities/backgrounds represent a stereotype, or did the author include intersectional representation?

Would you recommend this book? Who to?

Did the book make you want to meet the author?

What would you ask the author?

Some books are so familiar that reading them is like being home again.

Louisa May Alcott

LOUISA MAY ALCOTT

BOOK NO.:

PAGES:

TITLE:

AUTHOR:

RATING: ☆ ☆ ☆ ☆ ☆

START DATE:

GENRE:

FINISH DATE:

FORMAT:

FAVORITE QUOTES:

FIVE-WORD REVIEW:

Thoughts/Notes

Book Log

BOOK NO.:

PAGES:

TITLE:

AUTHOR:

RATING: ☆ ☆ ☆ ☆ ☆

START DATE:

GENRE:

FINISH DATE:

FORMAT:

FAVORITE QUOTES:

FIVE-WORD REVIEW:

Thoughts/Notes

BOOK NO.:

PAGES:

TITLE:

AUTHOR:

RATING: ☆ ☆ ☆ ☆ ☆

START DATE:

GENRE:

FINISH DATE:

FORMAT:

FAVORITE QUOTES:

FIVE-WORD REVIEW:

Thoughts/ Notes

Book Log

BOOK NO.:

PAGES:

TITLE:

AUTHOR:

RATING: ☆ ☆ ☆ ☆ ☆

START DATE:

GENRE:

FINISH DATE:

FORMAT:

FAVORITE QUOTES:

FIVE-WORD REVIEW:

Thoughts/
Notes

Book Log

BOOK NO.:

PAGES:

TITLE:

AUTHOR:

RATING: ☆ ☆ ☆ ☆ ☆

START DATE:

GENRE:

FINISH DATE:

FORMAT:

FAVORITE QUOTES:

FIVE-WORD REVIEW:

Thoughts/Notes

Book Log

BOOK NO.:

PAGES:

TITLE:

AUTHOR:

RATING: ☆ ☆ ☆ ☆ ☆

START DATE:

GENRE:

FINISH DATE:

FORMAT:

FAVORITE QUOTES:

FIVE-WORD REVIEW:

Thoughts/Notes

Book Log

BOOK NO.:

PAGES:

TITLE:

AUTHOR:

RATING: ☆ ☆ ☆ ☆ ☆

START DATE:

GENRE:

FINISH DATE:

FORMAT:

FAVORITE QUOTES:

FIVE-WORD REVIEW:

Thoughts/ Notes

PRIDE AND PREJUDICE

JANE AUSTEN

I declare after all there is **no** enjoyment like reading! How much **sooner** one tires of anything than of a **book!**

Book Log

BOOK NO.:

PAGES:

TITLE:

AUTHOR:

RATING: ☆ ☆ ☆ ☆ ☆

START DATE:

GENRE:

FINISH DATE:

FORMAT:

FAVORITE QUOTES:

FIVE-WORD REVIEW:

Thoughts/Notes

Book Log

BOOK NO.:

PAGES:

TITLE:

AUTHOR:

RATING: ☆ ☆ ☆ ☆ ☆

START DATE:

GENRE:

FINISH DATE:

FORMAT:

FAVORITE QUOTES:

FIVE-WORD REVIEW:

Thoughts/Notes

Book Log

BOOK NO.:

PAGES:

TITLE:

AUTHOR:

RATING: ☆ ☆ ☆ ☆ ☆

START DATE:

GENRE:

FINISH DATE:

FORMAT:

FAVORITE QUOTES:

FIVE-WORD REVIEW:

Thoughts/
Notes

Book Log

BOOK NO.:

PAGES:

TITLE:

AUTHOR:

RATING: ☆ ☆ ☆ ☆ ☆

START DATE:

GENRE:

FINISH DATE:

FORMAT:

FAVORITE QUOTES:

FIVE-WORD REVIEW:

Thoughts/ Notes

Book Log

BOOK NO.:

PAGES:

TITLE:

AUTHOR:

RATING: ☆ ☆ ☆ ☆ ☆

START DATE:

GENRE:

FINISH DATE:

FORMAT:

FAVORITE QUOTES:

FIVE-WORD REVIEW:

Thoughts/Notes

Book Log

BOOK NO.:

PAGES:

TITLE:

AUTHOR:

RATING: ☆ ☆ ☆ ☆ ☆

START DATE:

GENRE:

FINISH DATE:

FORMAT:

FAVORITE QUOTES:

FIVE-WORD REVIEW:

Thoughts/Notes

My most
anticipated
reads...

Dream Authors Dinner Party

You've been invited to a dinner party. Which table do you choose to sit at?

L.M. Montgomery

Shakespeare

Anne Brontë

Alexandre Dumas

☐

Virginia Woolf

Oscar Wilde

Mary Shelley

Arthur Conan Doyle

☐

Sylvia Plath

F. Scott Fitzgerald

Maya Angelou

Thomas Hardy

Jane Austen

George Orwell

Louisa May Alcott

Charles Dickens

☐

Which authors just NEED to be seated together? Who do you need to separate to keep the peace?

Create your own dinner party...

You can **never** get a cup of tea **large** enough or a **book** **long** enough to suit me.

C. S. LEWIS

Quick-Fire Questions

FAVORITE CHILDHOOD BOOK:

BOOK THAT CHANGED YOUR LIFE:

BEST BOOK-TO-MOVIE ADAPTATION:

MOST UNDERRATED BOOK:

BOOK THAT IGNITED YOUR LOVE OF READING:

BOOK YOU RECOMMEND THE MOST OFTEN:

BOOK YOU COULDN'T FINISH:

BEST RECOMMENDATION FROM A FRIEND:

BOOK YOU WISH YOU COULD READ AGAIN FOR THE FIRST TIME:

BOOK YOU REREAD THE MOST:

Book Log

BOOK NO.:

PAGES:

TITLE:

AUTHOR:

RATING: ☆ ☆ ☆ ☆ ☆

START DATE:

GENRE:

FINISH DATE:

FORMAT:

FAVORITE QUOTES:

FIVE-WORD REVIEW:

Thoughts/
Notes

Book Log

BOOK NO.:

PAGES:

TITLE:

AUTHOR:

RATING: ☆ ☆ ☆ ☆ ☆

START DATE:

GENRE:

FINISH DATE:

FORMAT:

FAVORITE QUOTES:

FIVE-WORD REVIEW:

Thoughts/Notes

Book Log

BOOK NO.:

PAGES:

TITLE:

AUTHOR:

RATING: ☆ ☆ ☆ ☆ ☆

START DATE:

GENRE:

FINISH DATE:

FORMAT:

FAVORITE QUOTES:

FIVE-WORD REVIEW:

Book Log

BOOK NO.:

PAGES:

TITLE:

AUTHOR:

RATING: ☆ ☆ ☆ ☆ ☆

START DATE:

GENRE:

FINISH DATE:

FORMAT:

FAVORITE QUOTES:

FIVE-WORD REVIEW:

Thoughts/
Notes

BOOK NO.:

PAGES:

TITLE:

AUTHOR: RATING: ☆ ☆ ☆ ☆ ☆

START DATE: GENRE:

FINISH DATE: FORMAT:

FAVORITE QUOTES:

FIVE-WORD REVIEW:

Thoughts/Notes

Book Log

BOOK NO.:

PAGES:

TITLE:

AUTHOR: RATING: ☆ ☆ ☆ ☆ ☆

START DATE: GENRE:

FINISH DATE: FORMAT:

FAVORITE QUOTES:

FIVE-WORD REVIEW:

Thoughts/Notes

Book
Log

BOOK NO.:

PAGES:

TITLE:

AUTHOR:

RATING: ☆ ☆ ☆ ☆ ☆

START DATE:

GENRE:

FINISH DATE:

FORMAT:

FAVORITE QUOTES:

FIVE-WORD REVIEW:

Thoughts/Notes

Is it insomnia?
Or is it
just a good book and
no respect for
tomorrow?

Book Log

BOOK NO.:

PAGES:

TITLE:

AUTHOR:

START DATE:

FINISH DATE:

RATING: ☆ ☆ ☆ ☆ ☆

GENRE:

FORMAT:

FAVORITE QUOTES:

FIVE-WORD REVIEW:

Thoughts/Notes

Book Log

BOOK NO.:

PAGES:

TITLE:

AUTHOR:

RATING: ☆ ☆ ☆ ☆ ☆

START DATE:

GENRE:

FINISH DATE:

FORMAT:

FAVORITE QUOTES:

FIVE-WORD REVIEW:

Thoughts/Notes

Book Log

BOOK NO.:

PAGES:

TITLE:

AUTHOR:

RATING: ☆ ☆ ☆ ☆ ☆

START DATE:

GENRE:

FINISH DATE:

FORMAT:

FAVORITE QUOTES:

FIVE-WORD REVIEW:

Thoughts/Notes

BOOK NO.:

PAGES:

TITLE:

AUTHOR:

RATING: ☆ ☆ ☆ ☆ ☆

START DATE:

GENRE:

FINISH DATE:

FORMAT:

FAVORITE QUOTES:

FIVE-WORD REVIEW:

Thoughts/Notes

Book Log

BOOK NO.:

PAGES:

TITLE:

AUTHOR:

RATING: ☆ ☆ ☆ ☆ ☆

START DATE:

GENRE:

FINISH DATE:

FORMAT:

FAVORITE QUOTES:

FIVE-WORD REVIEW:

Thoughts/Notes

Book Log

BOOK NO.:

PAGES:

TITLE:

AUTHOR: **RATING:** ☆ ☆ ☆ ☆ ☆

START DATE: **GENRE:**

FINISH DATE: **FORMAT:**

FAVORITE QUOTES:

FIVE-WORD REVIEW:

Thoughts/ Notes

My favorite reads so far...

Favorite Quotes

With freedom,
books, flowers
and the moon,
who could
not be happy?

OSCAR WILDE

Genres

Do you mostly read one genre? That's cool!
Do you read lots of different genres? Also cool!
Reading widely can be very rewarding.
Think about what books you've loved and
what books you'd like to read.

My favorite books in these genres are:

ACTION/ADVENTURE:

CLASSICS:

CRIME/MYSTERY:

BIOGRAPHY/MEMOIR:

ROMANCE:

Books I'd like to read in these genres are:

ACTION/ADVENTURE:

CLASSICS:

CRIME/MYSTERY:

BIOGRAPHY/MEMOIR:

ROMANCE:

Book Log

BOOK NO.:

PAGES:

TITLE:

AUTHOR:

RATING: ☆ ☆ ☆ ☆ ☆

START DATE:

GENRE:

FINISH DATE:

FORMAT:

FAVORITE QUOTES:

FIVE-WORD REVIEW:

Book Log

BOOK NO.:

PAGES:

TITLE:

AUTHOR:

RATING: ☆ ☆ ☆ ☆ ☆

START DATE:

GENRE:

FINISH DATE:

FORMAT:

FAVORITE QUOTES:

FIVE-WORD REVIEW:

Thoughts/Notes

Book Log

BOOK NO.:

PAGES:

TITLE:

AUTHOR:

RATING: ☆ ☆ ☆ ☆ ☆

START DATE:

GENRE:

FINISH DATE:

FORMAT:

FAVORITE QUOTES:

FIVE-WORD REVIEW:

Thoughts/Notes

Book Log

BOOK NO.:

PAGES:

TITLE:

AUTHOR:

RATING: ☆ ☆ ☆ ☆ ☆

START DATE:

GENRE:

FINISH DATE:

FORMAT:

FAVORITE QUOTES:

FIVE-WORD REVIEW:

Thoughts/
Notes

Book Log

BOOK NO.:

PAGES:

TITLE:

AUTHOR:

RATING: ☆ ☆ ☆ ☆ ☆

START DATE:

GENRE:

FINISH DATE:

FORMAT:

FAVORITE QUOTES:

FIVE-WORD REVIEW:

Thoughts/Notes

Book Log

BOOK NO.:

PAGES:

TITLE:

AUTHOR:

RATING: ☆ ☆ ☆ ☆ ☆

START DATE:

GENRE:

FINISH DATE:

FORMAT:

FAVORITE QUOTES:

FIVE-WORD REVIEW:

Thoughts/Notes

Book Log

BOOK NO.:

PAGES:

TITLE:

AUTHOR:

RATING: ☆ ☆ ☆ ☆ ☆

START DATE:

GENRE:

FINISH DATE:

FORMAT:

FAVORITE QUOTES:

FIVE-WORD REVIEW:

Thoughts/Notes

Between
the pages
of a
book
is a
lovely place
to be.

Book Log

BOOK NO.:

PAGES:

TITLE:

AUTHOR:

RATING: ☆ ☆ ☆ ☆ ☆

START DATE:

GENRE:

FINISH DATE:

FORMAT:

FAVORITE QUOTES:

FIVE-WORD REVIEW:

Thoughts/
Notes

Book Log

BOOK NO.:

PAGES:

TITLE:

AUTHOR:

RATING: ☆ ☆ ☆ ☆ ☆

START DATE:

GENRE:

FINISH DATE:

FORMAT:

FAVORITE QUOTES:

FIVE-WORD REVIEW:

Thoughts/Notes

Book Log

BOOK NO.:

PAGES:

TITLE:

AUTHOR:

RATING: ☆ ☆ ☆ ☆ ☆

START DATE:

GENRE:

FINISH DATE:

FORMAT:

FAVORITE QUOTES:

FIVE-WORD REVIEW:

Thoughts/Notes

Book Log

BOOK NO.:

PAGES:

TITLE:

AUTHOR:

RATING: ☆ ☆ ☆ ☆ ☆

START DATE:

GENRE:

FINISH DATE:

FORMAT:

FAVORITE QUOTES:

FIVE-WORD REVIEW:

Thoughts/
Notes

Book Log

BOOK NO.:

PAGES:

TITLE:

AUTHOR:

RATING: ☆ ☆ ☆ ☆ ☆

START DATE:

GENRE:

FINISH DATE:

FORMAT:

FAVORITE QUOTES:

FIVE-WORD REVIEW:

Thoughts/Notes

Book Log

BOOK NO.:

PAGES:

TITLE:

AUTHOR:

RATING: ☆ ☆ ☆ ☆ ☆

START DATE:

GENRE:

FINISH DATE:

FORMAT:

FAVORITE QUOTES:

FIVE-WORD REVIEW:

Fictional destinations I'd like to visit...

Desert Island Books

You're stranded on a desert island. You have just enough battery left on your phone to put in an order with your favorite independent bookshop that happens to deliver to remote tropical islands. Priorities, right?! What books will get you through the months ahead?

Fictional Character Travel Party

Which group of companions will you choose for each adventure below? Create your own too!

A A witch has cursed your town, erasing the last chapter of every book in the library! You gather this motley crew and spend the night in the haunted house to undo this evil...

You have been chosen for a quest that will save the people of your land, taking you on a long and arduous adventure. Who else is in the fellowship?

C Word is that Lady Catherine de Bourgh is in possession of documents that call into question the entail on your father's estate and could enable you and your sisters to inherit Longbourn. Who will you take with you to Rosings Park to distract Lady Catherine while you search for them undetected?

WRITE YOUR OWN:

Sherlock Holmes

The Queen of Hearts

Dr. Jekyll

Elizabeth Bennet

Anne Shirley

Mr. Collins

Jane Eyre

Puck

Sam + Frodo

Jo March

Tinker Bell

Mr. Darcy

Where is human nature so weak as in the bookstore?

HENRY WARD
BEECHER

Book Log

BOOK NO.:

PAGES:

TITLE:

AUTHOR:

RATING: ☆ ☆ ☆ ☆ ☆

START DATE:

GENRE:

FINISH DATE:

FORMAT:

FAVORITE QUOTES:

FIVE-WORD REVIEW:

Thoughts/
Notes

Book Log

BOOK NO.:

PAGES:

TITLE:

AUTHOR:

RATING: ☆ ☆ ☆ ☆ ☆

START DATE:

GENRE:

FINISH DATE:

FORMAT:

FAVORITE QUOTES:

FIVE-WORD REVIEW:

Book Log

BOOK NO.:

PAGES:

TITLE:

AUTHOR:

RATING: ☆ ☆ ☆ ☆ ☆

START DATE:

GENRE:

FINISH DATE:

FORMAT:

FAVORITE QUOTES:

FIVE-WORD REVIEW:

Thoughts/Notes

Book Log

BOOK NO.:

PAGES:

TITLE:

AUTHOR:

RATING: ☆ ☆ ☆ ☆ ☆

START DATE:

GENRE:

FINISH DATE:

FORMAT:

FAVORITE QUOTES:

FIVE-WORD REVIEW:

Thoughts/Notes

Book
Log

BOOK NO.:

PAGES:

TITLE:

AUTHOR:

RATING: ☆ ☆ ☆ ☆ ☆

START DATE:

GENRE:

FINISH DATE:

FORMAT:

FAVORITE QUOTES:

FIVE-WORD REVIEW:

Thoughts/Notes

BOOK NO.:

PAGES:

TITLE:

AUTHOR:

RATING: ☆ ☆ ☆ ☆ ☆

START DATE:

GENRE:

FINISH DATE:

FORMAT:

FAVORITE QUOTES:

FIVE-WORD REVIEW:

Thoughts/Notes

BOOK NO.:

PAGES:

TITLE:

AUTHOR: **RATING:** ☆ ☆ ☆ ☆ ☆

START DATE: **GENRE:**

FINISH DATE: **FORMAT:**

FAVORITE QUOTES:

FIVE-WORD REVIEW:

May your shelves always overflow with books.

BOOK NO.:

PAGES:

TITLE:

AUTHOR: **RATING:** ☆ ☆ ☆ ☆ ☆

START DATE: **GENRE:**

FINISH DATE: **FORMAT:**

FAVORITE QUOTES:

FIVE-WORD REVIEW:

Thoughts/ Notes

Book Log

BOOK NO.:

PAGES:

TITLE:

AUTHOR:

RATING: ☆ ☆ ☆ ☆ ☆

START DATE:

GENRE:

FINISH DATE:

FORMAT:

FAVORITE QUOTES:

FIVE-WORD REVIEW:

Thoughts/
Notes

Book Log

BOOK NO.:

PAGES:

TITLE:

AUTHOR:

RATING: ☆ ☆ ☆ ☆ ☆

START DATE:

GENRE:

FINISH DATE:

FORMAT:

FAVORITE QUOTES:

FIVE-WORD REVIEW:

Thoughts/Notes

Book Log

BOOK NO.:

PAGES:

TITLE:

AUTHOR:

RATING: ☆ ☆ ☆ ☆ ☆

START DATE:

GENRE:

FINISH DATE:

FORMAT:

FAVORITE QUOTES:

FIVE-WORD REVIEW:

Thoughts/
Notes

Book Log

BOOK NO.:

PAGES:

TITLE:

AUTHOR:

RATING: ☆ ☆ ☆ ☆ ☆

START DATE:

GENRE:

FINISH DATE:

FORMAT:

FAVORITE QUOTES:

FIVE-WORD REVIEW:

Thoughts/
Notes

BOOK NO.:

PAGES:

TITLE:

AUTHOR:

RATING: ☆ ☆ ☆ ☆ ☆

START DATE:

GENRE:

FINISH DATE:

FORMAT:

FAVORITE QUOTES:

FIVE-WORD REVIEW:

Thoughts/
Notes

My Reading Profile

Has any of this changed since you started the book?

DATE:

MY FAVORITE BOOK:

_____

MY FAVORITE AUTHOR:

_____

MY FAVORITE GENRE:

_____

WHERE I READ:

_____

WHEN I READ:

_____

WHY I READ:

_____

Reading
Reflections

Think about the goals section at the start of the book. How did it go?

There's no wrong answer!

A room without
books is like
a body without
a soul.

ATTRIBUTED TO CICERO

Favorite Quotes

To Be
Read...

To Be
Read...

To Be
Read...

To Be Read...

With
thanks to:

Gemma Harbour and Jess Thomas—design and illustration

Louise Verity and Beth Horsley—content and planning

Special thanks to Rebecca Sheidler
for support and wisdom